Desert Fire

by Shirley Frederick • illustrations by Joy Hein

Harcourt Brace & Company

Orlando Atlanta Austin Boston San Francisco Chicago Dallas New York Toronto London

A rabbit lives in the desert.
She has fur like the desert
sand. Her name is Desert Fur.

Desert Fur has three children.
The first has curls in her fur.
Her name is Curl Fur.

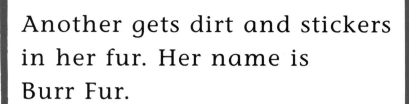

Another gets dirt and stickers
in her fur. Her name is
Burr Fur.

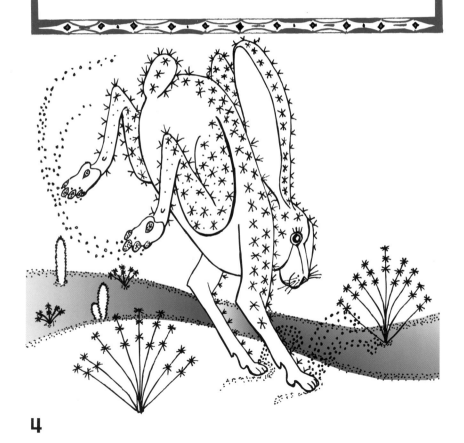

4

The third has fur like silver.
His name is Silver Fur.

One day while Silver Fur,
Burr Fur, and Curl Fur were
sleeping, Desert Fur left
to look for food.

Desert Fur smelled burning grass. "The desert is burning," she said to herself.

She turned to see a swirl
of smoke curling up. The
desert was a blur of smoke.

A bird chirped. "The desert is burning," said the bird.

The fire burned and burned.
It burned the cactus and the
desert grass.
"Run!" chirped the bird.

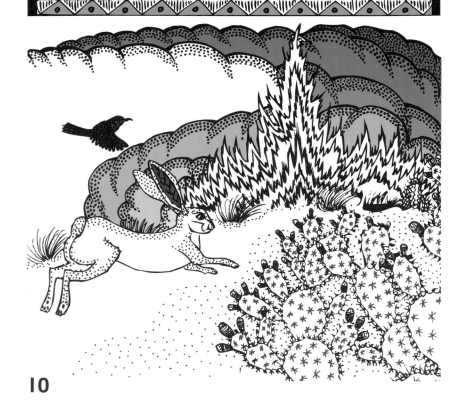

Desert Fur ran to Burr Fur,
Curl Fur, and Silver Fur. They
were not hurt.
"Run!" she said.

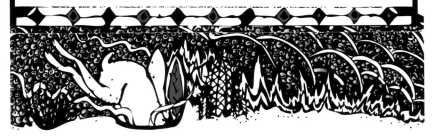

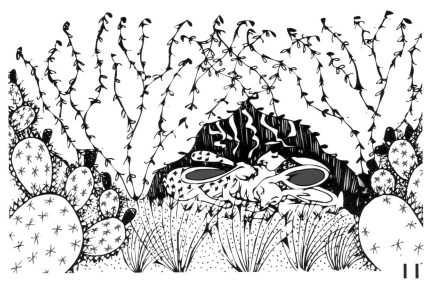

They all ran past the fir trees and down the mountain.
"Safe!" said Desert Fur.
"Safe!" chirped the bird.